PROFESSOR MURPHY'S
BRAIN-
BUSTING
PUZZLES
&
RIDDLES

This edition published by Parragon Books Ltd in 2015
and distributed by

Parragon Inc.
440 Park Avenue South, 13th Floor
New York, NY 10016
www.parragon.com

Copyright © Parragon Books Ltd 2015

Produced by Tall Tree Books

ISBN 978-1-4723-7656-5

Printed in China

PROFESSOR MURPHY'S
BRAIN-BUSTING
PUZZLES
&
RIDDLES

PaRragon

Bath · New York · Cologne · Melbourne · Delhi
Hong Kong · Shenzhen · Singapore · Amsterdam

CONTENTS

INTRODUCTION

Brain-Busting Puzzles & Riddles might sound like a daunting challenge to some people, but the collection of conundrums, problems, teasers, and mental hurdles in this book isn't designed to defeat you—they're all for fun!

They will, of course, make you think, and that will do you nothing but good. Scientists have shown that taking a little time to think about puzzles and riddles is good exercise for your mind. Just like the muscles in your body, the more you use your brain, the stronger it becomes, so you can have fun with this book and give your brain a workout at the same time.

People have been setting puzzles and riddles for thousands of years, although it shouldn't take you that long to figure out the answers to my brain busters, and I have compiled a varied selection of new posers and old favorites, including one of the oldest riddles of all time. Check the answers once you're finished to find out which one that is!

Prof WP Murphy

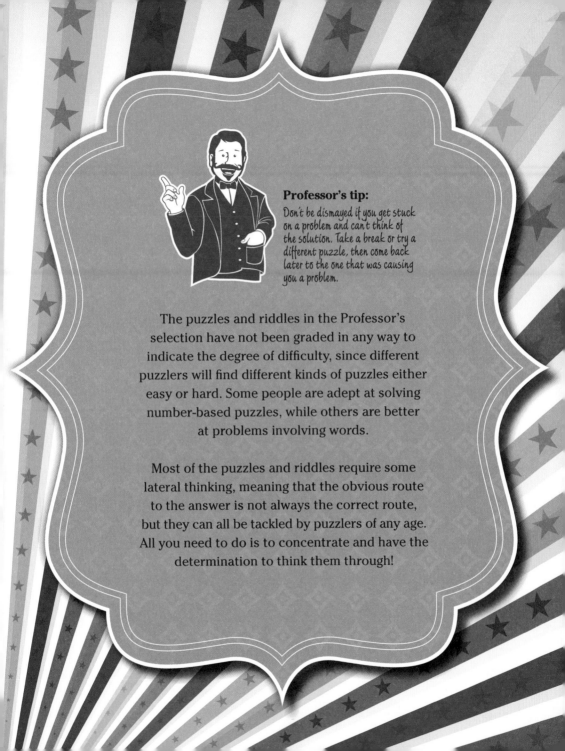

Professor's tip:

Don't be dismayed if you get stuck on a problem and can't think of the solution. Take a break or try a different puzzle, then come back later to the one that was causing you a problem.

The puzzles and riddles in the Professor's selection have not been graded in any way to indicate the degree of difficulty, since different puzzlers will find different kinds of puzzles either easy or hard. Some people are adept at solving number-based puzzles, while others are better at problems involving words.

Most of the puzzles and riddles require some lateral thinking, meaning that the obvious route to the answer is not always the correct route, but they can all be tackled by puzzlers of any age. All you need to do is to concentrate and have the determination to think them through!

GLASS TEASER

Six glasses are standing in a row.
The first three have water in them, but the
second three are empty. How can you make
the row of glasses alternate between full and
empty when you are only allowed to touch
or move one glass?

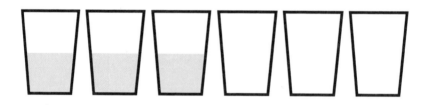

Professor's tip:
The rule is that you are only allowed to touch one glass, but
what you do with it when you are moving it is up to you!

Solution on p. 110

HAPPY FAMILY

Mr. and Mrs. Smith have six daughters.
If each daughter has one brother,

HOW MANY CHILDREN ARE IN THE FAMILY?

Solution on p. 110

LESS IS MORE

The more you have, the longer you'll live;
but the more you have had, the less
you have left.

—— WHAT ARE THEY? ——

Solution on p. 110

CUP CONUNDRUM

How can you put ten counters into three cups, so that each cup contains an odd number of counters?

Solution on p. 110

Checkmate

Two friends play chess once a week. Last week, they played five games. Each won as many games as the other, but no games ended in a tie, and no games were left unfinished.

HOW CAN THIS BE **?**

Solution on p. 110

LABEL MIX-UP

6

Harry has three boxes of fruit on his market stall. He has one box containing only apples, one box containing only pears, and one box with a mixture of apples and pears. There is a label on each box describing the contents, but none of the labels is on the correct box.

HOW CAN HARRY FIGURE OUT WHAT IS IN EACH BOX BY TAKING JUST ONE PIECE OF FRUIT FROM ONE BOX

Solution on p. 110

FIVE FINALISTS

7

Five friends run a race. Alan finished after Simon. Ian finished after Kevin. Simon finished after Brian. Kevin finished before Alan. Brian finished after Kevin. Brian finished before Alan. Simon finished before Ian. Alan finished before Ian.

WHO FINISHED WHERE

Solution on p. 110

STAYING DRY

8

Ten people are meeting at a restaurant, walking from three different directions. Only one of them has an umbrella, but they all arrive at the same time, and none of them gets wet.

HOW DID THEY MANAGE IT ?

Solution on p. 110

TOPSY-TURVY

9

How do you turn this shape upside down by moving only two lines?

Solution on p. 111

10

NEW BALLS, PLEASE!

A boy and a girl are both carrying baskets of tennis balls.
The girl says to the boy, "If I give you one of my tennis balls,
we will have the same. But if you give me one of yours,
I will have twice as many as you."

HOW MANY DID EACH HAVE ?

Solution on p. 111

ON TOP OF THE WORLD

11

Mount Everest, the highest mountain in the world,
was conquered in 1953 by New Zealander Sir Edmund
Hillary and Nepalese Sherpa Tenzing Norgay.

What was the highest mountain in the world
before Mount Everest was discovered?

Professor's tip:
You don't have to be a professor of history to consider
what was different about the world before 1953.

Solution on p. 111

LADDER JUMPER

How can you jump off a 35-foot
ladder onto solid concrete and
not hurt yourself?

Solution on p. 111

The Sock Drawer

You have 10 black socks and 12 white socks in a drawer,
but they are all mixed up, none of them together in pairs.
How many times do you have to reach into the drawer
and pull out a sock, without looking,

TO END UP WITH TWO MATCHING SOCKS **?**

Solution on p. 111

NUMBER JUMBLER

Using only digits 1 to 9, just once each, how can you make three numbers, each of three digits, where the second number is twice the first number and the third number is

____ THREE TIMES THE FIRST NUMBER **?** ____

Solution on p. 111

LUCKY WINNERS

Two fathers and two sons win a fortune on the lottery and go out together to buy new cars. They buy three brand-new luxury cars—one car each.

HOW CAN THIS BE **?**

Solution on p. 111

Movie Treats

16

James, Dominic, and Sarah are watching a movie together and sharing some chocolates. James can eat 27 chocolates in one hour. Sarah can eat 2 chocolates in 10 minutes. Dominic can eat 7 chocolates in 20 minutes.

HOW LONG WILL IT TAKE THEM TO EAT THE WHOLE BOX OF 120 CHOCOLATES

Solution on p. 111

17

MATTER OF TASTE

What will always taste better than it smells?

Solution on p. 112

SHELF SNACK

A three-part encyclopedia is sitting on a bookshelf. There are 300 pages in each volume. A bookworm chews its way from the first page of Volume 1 to the last page of Volume 3. Not counting covers, how many pages has it burrowed through?

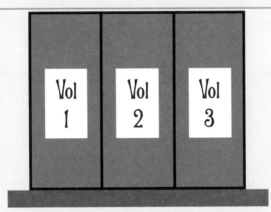

Professor's tip:
Think about the way the books sit on the shelf and where the hungry bookworm starts munching its way through them.

Solution on p. 112

19

MYSTERY OBJECT

I am made of solid wood, but if I drop on your foot, it won't hurt.
You can stand on me and I will not break. You can pick me up
very easily, but I cannot be cut with a saw.

—— WHAT AM I ——

Solution on p. 112

20

Give and Take

Taking me for yourself can be brave, but
giving me to someone to whom I do not
belong is wrong.

—— WHAT AM I ——

Solution on p. 112

TWIN TROUBLE

21

Two girls are born to the same mother at the same time, on the same day, in the same year, yet they are not twins.

— WHY IS THIS —

Solution on p. 112

FRUITY PROBLEM

22

A teacher, Miss Turner, has 11 children in her class. In a bowl on her desk, there are 11 apples. Miss Turner divides the apples among the class, so that each of her students has a whole apple, but there is one left in the bowl.

HOW CAN SHE DO THIS

Solution on p. 112

23

Less Is More

The more of these you take, the more
you leave behind

—— **WHAT ARE THEY** ? ——

Solution on p. 112

24

IN THE HOLE

How much soil is in a round hole
with a circumference of 35 feet and a
depth of 35 feet?

Professor's tip:
Think about the work you have to do to dig a
hole and what that work involves, no matter
how big the hole might be.

Solution on p. 112

SPOTS BEFORE YOUR EYES

Take a look at the nine spots shown on this page. Your challenge is to connect all of the spots using just four straight lines—and to make things even more difficult, you have to do it without lifting your pen from the paper.

○ ○ ○

○ ○ ○

○ ○ ○

Solution on p. 112

26

FAMILY TIES

Sharon is John's daughter.
This means that John is the
_____ of Sharon's father.

Solution on p. 112

27

Crisscross

What is the maximum number of Xs you
can draw on this tic-tac-toe board
without making three in a row in any direction?

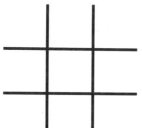

Solution on p. 113

AROUND THE WORLD

Imagine that you could lay a piece of string on the ground that stretched all the way around the world. The circumference of the Earth is about 25,000 miles. You must assume that your piece of string is lying on a flat surface all the way around.

Now imagine that you have an army of people standing on your piece of string. They are holding a second piece of string, and each of them is holding it exactly one foot above the ground. This second piece of string, therefore, circles the Earth one foot above the surface. How much longer must the second piece of string be?

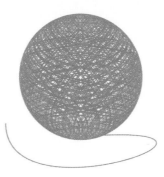

Solution on p. 113

Professor's tip:
If you have looked at the radius of a circle during class, then you should be able to figure out that the second piece of string needn't be as long as you might first expect.

ANGRY SHEEP

A farmer has ten very bad–tempered sheep that he keeps
in a circular paddock. The sheep cause a problem
when they start fighting with each other, so he has to
separate them. He has three circular fences that he can use
to keep them apart. The fences can intersect each other,
but how does he arrange the fences so that each of his
ten sheep is fenced off from all of the others?

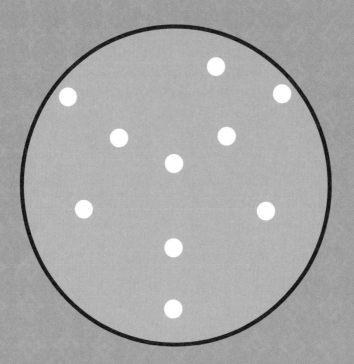

Solution on p. 113

THE GREAT 38

Can you place the numbers from 1 to 19 in the circles,
so that the numbers in each line add up to 38?

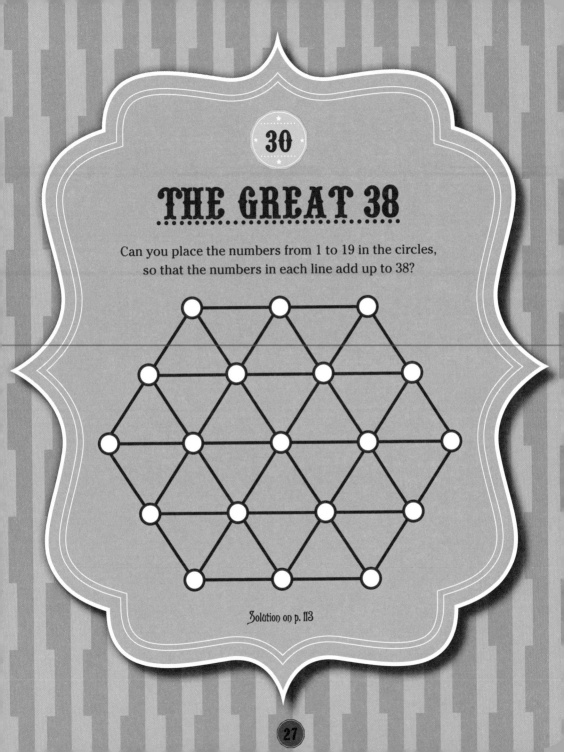

Solution on p. 113

SQUAWK OF TRUTH

A young man was invited to a party in the palace of an Arabian prince, and there he met the most beautiful girl he had ever seen. From the moment he was introduced to her, he was in love. As they strolled through the palace gardens, they heard a voice saying, "You look lovely!" They turned to see a brightly colored parrot perched on the branch of a tree. The young woman thought that the talking parrot, with its fantastic plumage and sassy speech, was simply wonderful.

The next day, the young man went to the great bazaar in town, determined to buy a parrot like the one at the palace. It was to be a gift for the young woman, to help him win her heart. He found a merchant who was selling a parrot almost identical to the one in the prince's palace. When he asked if the parrot could talk, the merchant promised him, "This parrot will repeat every word it hears." The young man immediately bought the parrot and spent the next few days trying to teach the bird to say, "I love you," but the parrot uttered not a single word. The young man took the parrot back to the bazaar and complained to the merchant that the bird would not talk, yet the merchant claimed he was being completely truthful when he said that the bird would repeat every word it heard.

HOW COULD —— HE HAVE BEEN TELLING THE TRUTH **?**——

Professor's tip:
Being able to talk is not always as valuable
a skill as being able to listen.

Solution on p. 113

32

THE NAME GAME

David's mother had three children.
The first child was named April;
the second child was named May;
what was the third child's name?

Solution on p. 114

33

CREATE 100

Using the same number between 1 and 9
and any of these mathematical symbols

$$(\div, +, -, \times),$$

create a calculation that equals 100.

Solution on p. 114

Butterfingers

If you drop me I am sure to crack,
but smile at me, and I will smile back.

— WHAT AM I **?** —

Solution on p. 114

SEVEN SPOTS

How can you arrange these seven black
spots so that there are six rows with
three spots in each row?

Professor's tip:
*Equal rows don't always
mean a square grid.*

Solution on p. 114

TRIANGLE OF TEN

Reverse this triangle of ten
counters by moving three.

Solution on p. 114

37

GONE IN A MOMENT

As soon as you talk about me, I am gone. Even saying my name will always make me disappear, and you can say nothing to make me return.

—— WHAT AM I——

Solution on p. 114

38

High Jump

What creature can jump
higher than a building?

Professor's tip:
It's not how high the creature can jump
that makes the real difference here!

Solution on p. 114

STRANGE GUESTS

They arrive in the evening without invitation and leave in the morning without saying goodbye.

___ **WHO ARE THESE STRANGE GUESTS**  ___

Solution on p. 114

GIANT PROBLEM

Two tribes of giants have been at war for many years but decide to have a peace conference. Each tribe sends 20 of its tallest giants to the conference. Because they are giants, they like to be tallest and will only shake hands with others who are smaller than themselves.

___ **HOW MANY SHAKE HANDS**  ___

Solution on p. 114

TOUGH TRIANGLES

These two triangles are formed using a total of six toothpicks. The challenge is to use only the same six toothpicks to form four triangles, all of an equal size.

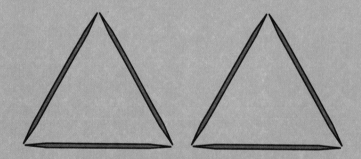

Solution on p. 114

PIRATE PUZZLE

Two pirate ships, one captained by Cutlass Jake and the other by Skeleton Pete, arrive at a desert island. Both pirate captains have identical treasure maps, and they rush ashore to find the hidden loot. Eventually, they reach an ancient rock beneath which two treasure chests have been buried. One chest is half full of gold doubloons, while the other is half full of worthless lead disks that weigh the same as the gold.

They argue over the gold, and both pirates and their crews have swords and pistols drawn, ready to fight. They know that if a battle breaks out, none of them may survive, so Skeleton Pete suggests that he should divide the gold and the lead between the two chests. Cutlass Jake can then blindfold him and mix up the chests, so that he does not know which is which. Pete will then pick one piece from one of the chests. If he chooses gold, he gets to keep all of the gold, and his crew is rich. If he chooses lead, he gets the lead, and Jake's crew takes all the gold.

How does Skeleton Pete divide the gold and the lead between the two chests to give himself the best chance of choosing gold?

Solution on p. 115

Professor's tip:
Here's a clue that might help. Skeleton Pete has to divide the gold and the lead between the two chests, but he doesn't necessarily have to divide it evenly ...

SKETCH CHALLENGE

Can you recreate this shape without lifting your pen off the paper and without going over the same line twice?

Solution on p. 115

Nobody's Son

I am a father's child and a mother's child, yet I am no one's son.

WHY?

Solution on p. 115

CAN YOU SEE?

The more there is of me,
the less you can see.

— WHAT AM I ? —

Solution on p. 115

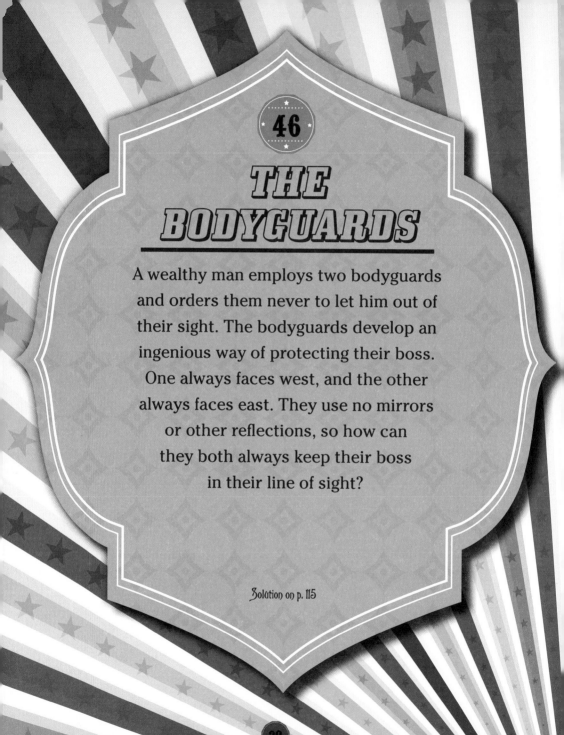

THE BODYGUARDS

A wealthy man employs two bodyguards and orders them never to let him out of their sight. The bodyguards develop an ingenious way of protecting their boss. One always faces west, and the other always faces east. They use no mirrors or other reflections, so how can they both always keep their boss in their line of sight?

Solution on p. 115

OVERTAKING

If you overtake the person in
second place in a race,

WHAT
— POSITION ARE **?** —
YOU NOW IN

Solution on p. 115

SHORT IS BIG

The shorter I am, the bigger and
more frightening I am.

— WHAT AM I **?** —

Solution on p. 115

THE HAIRDRESSERS

A cowboy rides into a small Western town that he has never visited before. He has come to meet with an important rancher who wants to hire a foreman for his ranch. The cowboy wants to make a good impression, so he checks into the only hotel in town, takes a bath, dresses in his best clothes, and goes out to get his hair cut. There are only two barbers in town—one near the saloon and one near the stables. The barber who has his shop near the saloon looks perfectly groomed, with immaculate hair. The barber whose shop is near the stables looks very shaggy, with unevenly cut hair. Which barber should the cowboy visit to get the best haircut and why?

Professor's tip:
Remember, appearances can be deceptive.

Solution on p. 115

THE BANK JOB

Four robbers tunnel their way into a bank vault, where they know that they will find lots of bags full of money. The tunnel is very narrow, and there is only room for one of them to enter the vault at a time. They agree that they will each take half of whatever they find in the vault. The first robber enters, takes half the bags, but because he is basically dishonest, he also takes one more. The second robber is just as dishonest as the first and takes half of what he finds, plus one. The third robber does the same, and when the fourth robber goes into the vault, there are no bags of money left at all. How many bags had been there originally?

Solution on p. 115

Long Weekend

A traveler on a long journey rides into a small town in the heart of the prairie.

He rides in on Friday and checks in to the only hotel in town. He stays for three nights, then rides out again on Friday.

___ HOW CAN **?** ___
THIS BE

Solution on p. 116

IT'S BEHIND YOU!

What is always behind you but never more than a day away?

Professor's tip:
Sometimes the answer to a question like this is much more obvious than you might think.

Solution on p. 116

NUMBER SQUARE

The digits 1, 2, 3, 4, 5, 6, 7, 8, and 9 must be put in this square in such a way that the sums of the numbers in each row, column, and diagonal are equal.

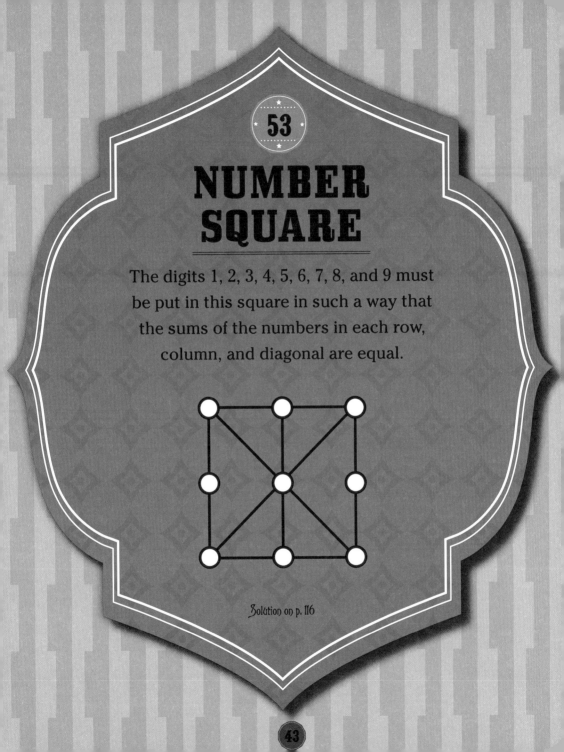

Solution on p. 116

Stair Race

I run upstairs ahead of you and always reach the bottom of the stairs before you.

— WHAT AM I **?** —

Solution on p. 116

A FUNNY AGE

A girl was 14 on her last birthday and will be 16 on her next.

— HOW IS THIS POSSIBLE **?** —

Solution on p. 116

56

A PIECE OF CAKE

How do you divide a circular birthday cake
into eight equal pieces using only three
straight cuts and without moving any pieces?

Solution on p. 116

57

BIG BREAK

What has to be broken before
you can use it?

Professor's tip:
I can promise you, without breaking my promise,
that some people break these every day!

Solution on p. 116

58

BORDER DILEMMA

Why can't a man living in Canada
be legally buried in the United States?

Solution on p. 116

59

Never Share

If you have one, you can keep it
forever, but if you share one,
it will no longer exist.

— WHAT IS IT—

Solution on p. 116

THE COWBOYS' HATS 60

Three cowboys rode into a town in the Wild West.
One had a black horse and wore brown boots.
One had a white horse and wore black boots.
One had a brown horse and wore white boots.

___ WHICH ONE WORE THE BIGGEST HAT ? ___

Solution on p. 116

ONE-WAY 61

A policeman sees that a bus driver is going against the traffic down a one-way street but does not stop him.

WHY NOT ?

Solution on p. 117

TWIN FIBS

Twins Billy and Tom are in the same class at school. Both are known to tell fibs, but Billy only lies on Monday, Tuesday, and Wednesday—the rest of the week he tells the truth. Tom only lies on Thursday, Friday, and Saturday—the rest of the week he tells the truth.

Billy says: "Yesterday I was lying."
Tom says: "So was I."

WHO IS TELLING THE TRUTH

Solution on p. 117

63

UPS AND DOWNS

What can go up a chimney down
but not down a chimney up?

Solution on p. 117

STRANGE PLACES 64

Where can you find rivers with no fish,
roads with no cars, seas with no ships,
and towns with no people?

Professor's tip:
This sounds like a real disaster, but it's more likely to
help get you out of trouble than to land you in it.

Solution on p. 117

SNAIL'S PACE

A snail is at the bottom of a well that is 20 bricks deep. Every day, the snail climbs 5 bricks up the side of the well, but every night, it slides back 4 bricks again.

___ WHAT DAY DOES IT REACH THE TOP ___

Solution on p. 117

No Questions Asked

What asks no questions but must always be answered?

Professor's tip:
Thinking of home might ring a bell.

Solution on p. 117

MISSING LETTERS

What are the next three letters
in the following sequence?

JFM AMJ JAS ---

Solution on p. 117

THE READER

A man sits by a window reading. No light is switched on in
the room, there is no moon outside, and he has no flashlight,
lamp, or candle, yet he can still see to read.

HOW IS THIS POSSIBLE

Solution on p. 117

NUMBER CIRCLES

The numbers 1 to 16 must be placed in the circles of the square below in such a way that the sum of the numbers in each row, column, and diagonal amounts to 34.

HOW SHOULD THE ── NUMBERS BE ARRANGED ── IN THE SQUARE

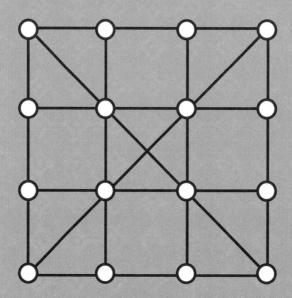

Solution on p. 117

UPTURNED GLASSES

These seven glasses are all in a row and all upside down. Your challenge is to turn them all right way up in the least possible moves. You must always turn over three glasses in one move.

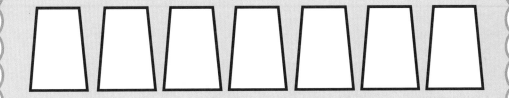

___ **HOW MANY MOVES ARE REQUIRED** ? ___

Professor's tip:
When you have turned a glass over, it needn't stay that way.

Solution on p. 118

DROWNING IN SOCKS

You have a really mixed-up sock drawer that is stuffed full of different-colored socks. You have 2 red, 4 yellow, 6 purple, 8 brown, 10 white, 12 green, 14 black, 16 blue, 18 gray, and 20 orange socks. Without looking, how many socks do you need to take out of the drawer to be sure that you have at least three pairs of socks of the same color?

Solution on p. 118

How Many Aunts?

How many aunts do I have if all of them except two live in New York, and all of them except two live in Paris, and all of them except two live in London?

Solution on p. 118

HALF A GLASS

You have a glass of water that you think is half full. Assuming that the glass is a perfect cylinder, and using no other implements or instruments, how can you tell accurately if the glass is half full?

Solution on p. 118

NEVER YES

To what question can the answer never be

"YES?"

Solution on p. 118

MYSTERY OBJECT

I cannot talk. I cannot walk or crawl. I come into a room, but I never sit on the furniture, yet I never leave.

—WHAT AM I?—

Solution on p. 118

WHAT'S MISSING?

What is the missing part of this sequence?

16 06 68 88 ?? 98

Solution on p. 118

DAYS GONE BY

77

When the day after tomorrow is yesterday, today will be as far from Wednesday as today was from Wednesday when the day before yesterday was tomorrow.

—— WHAT IS TOMORROW ? ——

Solution on p. 118

78

FAMILY FUN

At a family party, a grandfather, a grandmother, two fathers, two mothers, four children, three grandchildren, one brother, two sisters, two sons, two daughters, one father-in-law, one mother-in-law, and one daughter-in-law sit at a table.

—— HOW MANY PEOPLE ARE AT THE TABLE?

Solution on p. 119

79

Walk On By

It walks on four legs in the morning, two legs at noon, and three legs in the evening.

—— WHAT IS IT? ——

Solution on p. 119

Professor's tip:
This is one of the world's most ancient riddles, and the answer may seem strange to us in the modern world. It is an interesting riddle, nevertheless.

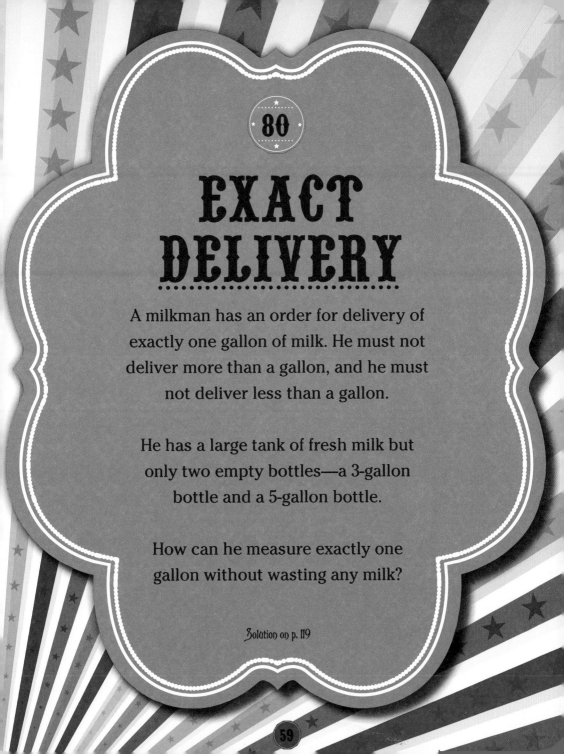

EXACT DELIVERY

A milkman has an order for delivery of exactly one gallon of milk. He must not deliver more than a gallon, and he must not deliver less than a gallon.

He has a large tank of fresh milk but only two empty bottles—a 3-gallon bottle and a 5-gallon bottle.

How can he measure exactly one gallon without wasting any milk?

Solution on p. 119

The Farmer's Son

One morning when he goes to collect the eggs from the chicken coop, a farmer's son finds a young fox that has become caught in some wire while trying to get at the chickens in the coop. The fox is not badly injured but it is frightened and exhausted, as it has been struggling to free itself for hours.

The boy calms the fox and frees it from the wire but when the farmer spots the fox, he orders his son to kill it. Foxes are not welcome on farms, after all, even if they are only young and small. The fox seems so harmless and cute that the boy hides it, intending to keep it as a pet.

Later that morning, the farmer sends his son to the market with a sack of corn and a chicken to sell. The boy takes the fox as well, smuggling it inside his jacket. To reach the market, he has to cross a river using a small raft. There is room on the raft for only him and one other thing.

This poses a real problem. If he takes the fox across the river first, he must leave the chicken and the corn. The chicken will then eat the corn. If he takes the chicken across the river, he must go back for the fox and leave the fox with the chicken when he returns for the corn. The fox will then eat the chicken.

Clearly, he can't leave the chicken with the corn or the fox with the chicken. He thinks about it for a while, then comes up with a solution that will get them all safely across the river.

HOW DOES HE DO IT ?

Solution on p. 119

82

MEET AND GREET

A mother and her daughter are walking down the street
when they meet a man, and both say, "Hello, Father."

HOW CAN THIS BE ?

Solution on p. 119

HARD WORKER

83

I am used from head to toe, and the
harder I work, the smaller I grow.

— WHAT AM I ? —

Professor's tip:
This hard worker may grow smaller but comes
in all different shapes and sizes.

Solution on p. 119

Toothpick Math

$$IX - IX = V$$

Move one toothpick
to correct the equation.

Solution on p. 119

Professor's tip:
You'll need to know your Roman
numerals to solve this problem.
Think where you can move your
toothpick to create a new numeral
—or change an existing one.

AGE IN NUMBERS

85

When asked how old he is, a child replies: "In four years, I will be twice as old as I was three years ago. And a year after that, I will be three times as old as I was five years ago."

___ HOW OLD ? ___
IS HE

Solution on p. 120

BIRTHDAY BRAIN BUSTER

86

Twin sisters each give birth to a son at exactly the same moment, yet the boys have different birthdays.

HOW CAN ?
THIS BE

Solution on p. 120

THE TRAVELER

As I was going to St. Ives,
I met a man with seven wives.
Each wife had seven sacks,
Each sack had seven cats,
Each cat had seven kits.
Kits, cats, sacks, wives,

HOW MANY WERE GOING TO ST. IVES ?

Professor's tip:
To solve this riddle, think about what it's actually telling you—not what you think it's telling you!

Solution on p. 120

ANCIENT WONDER

I am as old as the world but new every month.

—— WHAT AM I **?** ——

Solution on p. 120

CRASH MYSTERY

Two cars parked on the same one-lane road, one mile apart, set off at the same time, traveling at 60 mph, one heading east and one heading west. There was no room for them to pass or even for them to swerve to avoid each other, yet they did not crash into each other.

—— WHY **?** ——

Solution on p. 120

BACKWARD FISH

Can you move just three toothpicks to make this toothpick fish swim the other way?

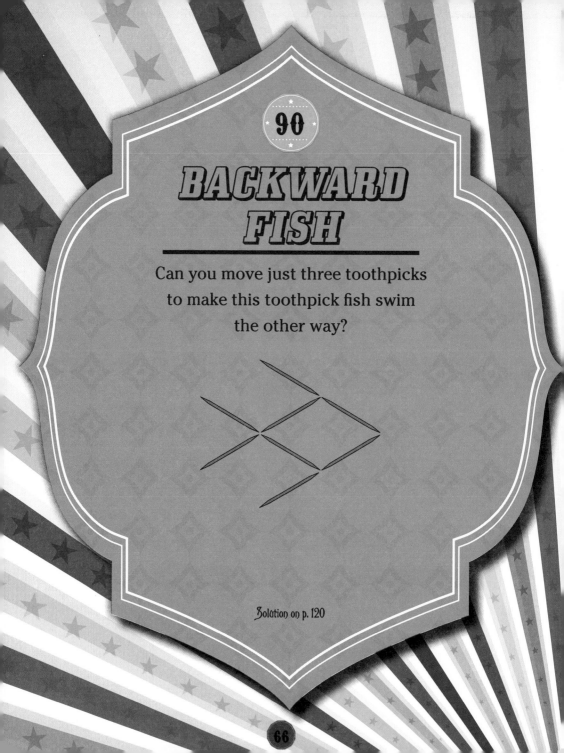

Solution on p. 120

IT'S ALL YOURS

What belongs to you, but others use
it more than you do?

Professor's tip:
Try to think about all the things that
are yours, not just things you buy.

Solution on p. 120

STAYING ALOFT

What is up with the birds and goes
around above the trees all day without
ever touching a leaf or landing on
a branch or twig?

Solution on p. 120

CHESS PROBLEM

How many squares are on a chessboard?
If you think that the answer is 64,
then think again!

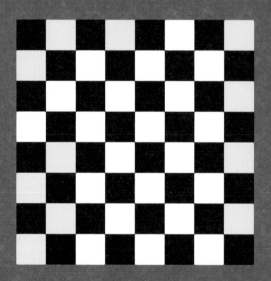

Solution on p. 121

94

MENTAL ARITHMETIC

TRY this equation by figuring it out IN YOUR HEAD without using a pencil and paper or any kind of calculator.
Take 1,000 and add 40 to it. Now add another 1,000 to it. Now add 30. And another 1,000. Now add 20. Now add another 1,000. Now add 10.

WHAT'S YOUR TOTAL

Solution on p. 121

LATE ARRIVAL?

95

What is always on its way but never actually gets here?

Professor's tip:
You might think the answer is travel-related, but think carefully: What else can be "on its way?"

Solution on p. 121

HIDE-AND-SEEK

Is it true when people say that when they lose something, they always find it in the last place they would think of looking?

Solution on p. 121

Ups and Downs

This is something that will always go up but will never come down.

 — **WHAT IS IT** —

Professor's tip:
Don't get frustrated if you don't get the answer right away.
This riddle will take a little bit of lateral thinking to solve.

Solution on p. 121

SON OF MY FATHER

A father and his young son are on a long train trip and the boy's father goes to the dining car to buy them some sandwiches. He has their tickets in his wallet. While he is gone, a conductor and a police officer come walking through the car. The boy has no ticket to show them, but the police officer says to the conductor, "Don't worry, this boy is my son."

HOW CAN THAT BE TRUE **?**

Solution on p. 121

99

LOVE AND MARRIAGE

He has married many women, but
he has never had a wife.

WHO IS HE

Solution on p. 121

100

UNTOUCHABLE

You can see me but not touch me.
Put me in a bucket, and I will make it lighter.

—— WHAT AM I ? ——

Solution on p. 121

THE CASTLE GUARD

In a land where three kings were at war over who owned some territory that bordered each of their kingdoms, a guard on night duty in the castle of one of the kings had a strange dream in which he saw the armies of the other two kings attacking at dawn.

He went to his king and told him that, in his dream, he had seen the armies of the other kings coming from the east as the sun rose. The king ordered his army to prepare to defend the castle. At dawn, just as the guard had said, the enemy forces appeared. Because the army had set up its defenses, the attackers were repelled, and everyone in the castle was saved.

The king then demanded to see the guard who had told him of the attack and had him thrown in the dungeon.

WHY DID HE DO THIS ?

Solution on p. 121

102

SOMETHING TO BE KEPT

What can you only keep after you have first given it to someone else?

Solution on p. 121

103

Gripping Problem

They have no flesh, they have no bone, yet they have fingers and thumbs of their own.

___ WHAT ARE THEY ? ___

Solution on p. 121

CATCH ME IF YOU CAN

You can catch me but not throw me.

— WHAT AM I —

Solution on p. 122

FIND MY HOME

I come in different shapes and sizes. Parts of me are curved, other parts are straight. You can keep me anywhere you like, but there is only one place where you need me to be.

— WHAT AM I —

Solution on p. 122

STRANGE SCENE

106

While walking past a house, you find a strange collection of things on the ground—nine lumps of coal, a carrot, a scarf, and two broken twigs.

_____ WHO DO YOU THINK LEFT _____
THEM THERE

Solution on p. 122

HOLD ON

107

What is as light as a feather but cannot be held for ten minutes by even the strongest of men?

Professor's tip:
The key word in this riddle is "held."
Make a mental list of the various things that you can hold.

Solution on p. 122

THE LOSER WINS

A very wealthy Arab sheikh was growing old and knew that he did not have many years left to live. He had two sons who argued with each other over everything. The old sheikh knew that his sons would argue over his money after he was dead, so he decided that he must put one of them in charge. The son who was put in charge would have to promise to split the old sheikh's wealth evenly with his brother.

The sons had identical Ferrari sports cars, so to decide who should be in charge after his death, the old sheikh set them a challenge. They had to race to a town many miles away, but the winner would be the one whose car took longest to reach the town.

The brothers were stumped. How could they stage a race where you had to go slowest to win? For once, they agreed on something—they needed help to figure out this problem. They drove their Ferraris to a tent where a wise man lived. After they had explained their problem, the wise man gave them some advice, whereupon the brothers rushed from the tent and sped off in the Ferraris toward the distant town.

WHAT DID THE WISE MAN TELL THEM TO DO ?

Solution on p. 122

109

FAST OR SLOW

Which can outrun
you—cold or warmth?

Solution on p. 122

110

GLOBETROTTER

What can travel the world
while stuck in a corner?

Professor's tip:
*You may get a little "stuck" yourself on this riddle,
but what other kinds of thing can be stuck?*

Solution on p. 122

65 SQUARE

The numbers 1 up to 25 must be placed in the circles of the square below in such a way that the sum of the numbers in each row, column, and diagonal amounts to 65.

HOW SHOULD THE NUMBERS BE ARRANGED IN THE SQUARE

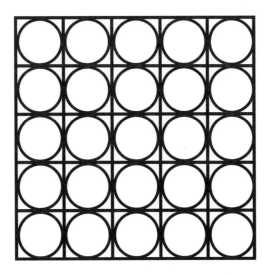

Solution on p. 122

112

A LIFE STORY

I am like a runner. I go fast if I am slim, but if I am fat,
I am slow. I am often seen with cake
but never eat any.

— WHAT AM I ? —

Solution on p. 122

113

WET OR DRY

What gets wetter
the more it dries?

Professor's tip:
Note that words often have
more than one meaning.

Solution on p. 123

MAKE A CENTURY

Below is an equation that is not correct yet. By adding a number of plus signs and minus signs between the digits on the left side (without changing the order of the digits), the equation can be made correct. 1 2 3 4 5 6 7 8 9 = 100.

HOW MANY WAYS CAN YOU COME UP WITH TO MAKE 100 ?

Solution on p. 123

115

FOOD AND DRINK

Feed me and I will live, but give me water and I will die.

— WHAT AM I **?** —

Solution on p. 123

116

Running nowhere

Split in two, just in time, standing still, I'm running fine.

— WHAT AM I **?** —

Professors tip:
This is a rhyming riddle, which should make it easier to remember if you need to think about it later.

Solution on p. 123

BEHIND EACH OTHER

Susan is standing behind Helen at the same time that Helen is standing behind Susan.

HOW IS THIS POSSIBLE?

Solution on p. 123

TAKE IT AWAY

How many times can you subtract

10 FROM 100?

Solution on p. 123

TRUTH OR FICTION?

One of these statements is not true.
Two of these statements are not true.
Three of these statements are not true.
Four of these statements are not true.
Five of these statements are not true.
Six of these statements are not true.
Seven of these statements are not true.
Eight of these statements are not true.
Nine of these statements are not true.
Ten of these statements are not true.

WHICH, IF ANY, OF —— THESE STATEMENTS IS ACTUALLY TRUE ——

Solution on p. 123

THE GIANT AND THE TROLL

A traveler is hiking through an enchanted forest when he meets an old woman who warns him to turn back. When he asks why, she says, "Ahead, the path divides, taking two routes through the trees. One path leads deep into the darkest part of the forest, where there lurk all manner of evil creatures. No man has ever returned from there alive. The other path leads to a castle where a fairy princess will grant you one wish. Whatever you desire can be yours—wealth, wisdom, or everlasting life.

"The way is guarded by a giant and a troll. Once they have you in their clutches, they will force you to choose one path. You may ask one question to either the giant or the troll, but be warned: One of them is sworn always to tell the truth while the other always tells nothing but lies."

"Excellent!" says the traveler. "Then I shall look forward to meeting the fairy princess!" And he sets off up the path. What question did the traveller intend to ask, and who did he ask—the giant or the troll?

Solution on p. 123

Professor's tip:
There are lots of characters and details in this story, but don't let them distract you. The answer is probably simpler than you think. Just concentrate on finding the "truth."

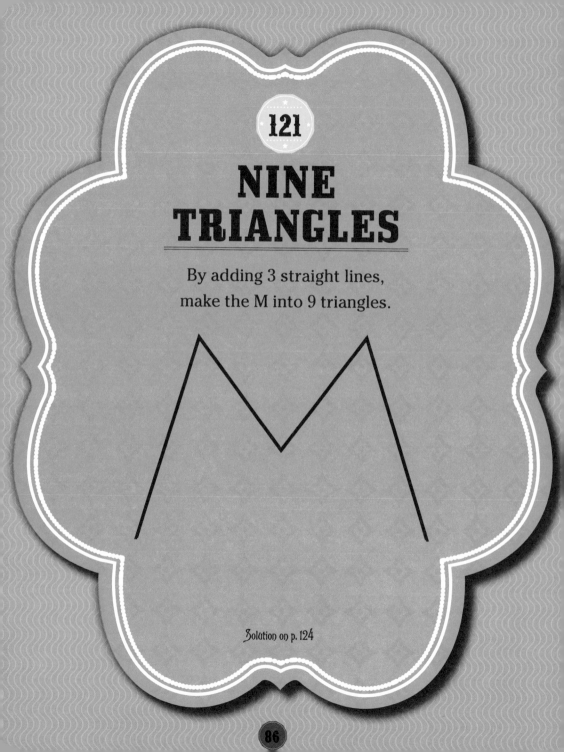

121

NINE TRIANGLES

By adding 3 straight lines,
make the M into 9 triangles.

Solution on p. 124

122

BRICK BUILDING

On a building site, 80 bricklayers lay 80,000 bricks in eight days. How many bricks do 40 bricklayers lay in

4 DAYS?

Solution on p. 124

123

FALL GUY

A man painting window frames on the top floor of his house slips and falls, yet he is completely unhurt.

WHY WAS HE NOT INJURED?

Solution on p. 124

124

BACKWARD NUMBER

What number less than 100 increases
by one-fifth of its value when
its digits are reversed?

Solution on p. 124

125

Day-to-Day

The day after tomorrow is the
third day after Wednesday.

WHAT WAS THE
DAY BEFORE
YESTERDAY

Solution on p. 124

HOURS AND MINUTES

With a 7-minute hourglass and an 11-minute hourglass, what is the simplest way to time exactly

—— 15 MINUTES ——

Solution on p. 124

WATER CARRIER

I have holes in my top and bottom,
my left and right, and in the middle.
But I still hold water.

—— WHAT AM I ——

Solution on p. 124

HORSE INCIDENT

A horse jumped over a tower and landed
on a man; the man disappeared.

WHAT JUST HAPPENED ?

Solution on p. 125

CONUNDRUM

I have an end but no beginning, a home but no family,
a space but no room. I can give any name, and there
is no word I can't produce, yet I never speak.

WHAT AM I ?

Solution on p. 125

GUIDE TEAMS

At a forest preserve, the volunteer guides will be organized into two teams for training, The Bear Team and The Eagle Team. Each guide has to have either an eagle or a bear button pinned to his or her hat. All of the guides have been allocated to a team except three—Jane, Freddy, and Mike. There are five buttons left—three eagles and two bears. For fun, Jane, Freddy, and Mike are blindfolded, and the others pin a button onto their hats. The remaining two buttons are then hidden, and Jane, Freddy, and Mike are allowed to remove their blindfolds.

The three have been positioned so that Jane can see Freddy and Mike's buttons, Mike can see Freddy's button, and Freddy can't see anyone's button.

When they are asked whether they have eagle or bear buttons, Jane says that she doesn't know, and Mike also says that he doesn't know.

Freddy says, "I'm in The Eagle Team!"
How did he know?

Solution on p. 125

131 Start Digging

If it takes one man three days to dig a hole,
how long would it take two men to dig

HALF A HOLE **?**

Solution on p. 125

132 LEWIS CARROLL'S RIDDLE

A stick I found that weighed two pounds:
I sawed it up one day.
In pieces eight of equal weight,
how much did each piece weigh?

Solution on p. 125

133

HEAVY BURDEN

Carrying my burden would break a rich man's back. I have no riches but can leave silver in my track.

— WHAT AM I—

Solution on p. 125

LETTER SEQUENCE

134

What comes next in this sequence?

— O T T F F S S—

Professor's tip:
Are these just random letters, or does each letter perhaps stand for something?

Solution on p. 125

135

STRANGE SPEARS

Shining, downward-thrusting spears that
shed no rust but sometimes tears.

WHAT ARE THEY ?

Solution on p. 126

136

COLORFUL HOUSES

Three single-story houses stood in a row—one blue, one pink, and
one green. Absolutely everything in the blue house, including the
carpets, curtains, furniture, and walls, was blue. Similarly, everything in
the pink house was pink, and everything in the green house was green.

WHAT COLOR WERE THE STAIRS IN THE BLUE HOUSE ?

Solution on p. 126

MAGIC BALL

A magician claims to be able to throw a ball so that it goes a short distance, stops, turns around, and comes back again, without him bouncing it off of any object or tying anything to the ball.

___ HOW DOES HE DO IT ?___

Solution on p. 126

NOT SO HANDY

138

I have hands, but they cannot grip. My hands can point, but they cannot clap.

— WHAT AM I ?—

Solution on p. 126

TRICKY TRIANGLE

How many triangles are in the image?

Solution on p. 126

SHADY CIRCLES

Fill in the white circles in such a way that the numbers in the boxes indicate how many dark circles surround them.

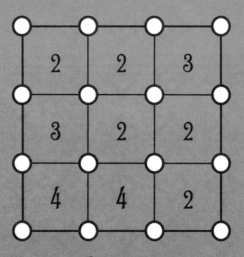

2 2 3

3 2 2

4 4 2

Solution on p. 126

141

IN A DAZE

A teacher asked a pupil if he could name three days of the week that come one after the other, but without using Tuesday, Friday, or Sunday.

WHAT DID HE SAY

Solution on p. 126

142

NO ESCAPE

An explorer out trekking alone comes across a bear and stops, standing stock-still. The bear doesn't see him and the explorer decides to make a run for it before the bear realizes that he is there.

In order to confuse the bear, should it follow his tracks, he runs a mile south, then a mile west, then a mile north. To his dismay, he finds the bear waiting for him, although the bear has not moved at all.

WHAT COLOR IS THE BEAR

Solution on p. 126/127

MISSING SYMBOLS

143

8 8 8 8 8 8 8 8 = 1,000. Using only addition symbols (+) between the eights, make this equation work.

Professor's tip:
It will probably take a little trial and error to find the solution to this problem.

Solution on p. 127

HALF GIRLS

144

A man has seven children.
Half of them are daughters.

HOW CAN THIS BE

Solution on p. 127

AMAZING NUMBER

Can you think of a number that has ten digits
and fits the following description?
The first digit is the number of zeros in the number.
The second digit is the number of ones.
The third digit is the number of twos.
The fourth digit is the number of threes.
The fifth digit is the number of fours.
The sixth digit is the number of fives.
The seventh digit is the number of sixes.
The eighth digit is the number of sevens.
The ninth digit is the number of eights.
The tenth digit is the number of nines.

Professor's tip:
This problem is not as
complicated as it might
look at first glance.

Solution on p. 127

HIS LORDSHIP'S ESTATE

A rich nobleman was lord of a vast estate that covered farmland, woodland, lakes, and hills. He had two children and decided that, in order to keep them from fighting over which parts of his land they should inherit, they should have half each, and they would all agree on how the land was to be divided.

Looking at a map, they quickly realized that the most valuable farmland was in several different areas and couldn't easily be divided without causing problems over access to water and access to roads.

His lordship eventually became weary of the long debate and tedious bickering, so he came up with a simple way to make sure that the children divided the land fairly between them and agreed on the solution.

____ HOW DID HE GET **?**____ THEM TO AGREE

Solution on p. 127

147 STRANGE OBJECT

I am not strong, yet the strongest door cannot stand
in my way. I am not rich, yet I can access things
of great value. I have no friends, yet people
will stand in the street to wait for me.

— WHAT AM I ? —

Solution on p. 127

148 WEIGHTY PROBLEM

You are handed a bag containing nine balls
that are identical in size, but one is slightly
heavier than the others. How many times do
you have to load a balance in order to find
out which is the heavy ball?

Solution on p. 127

149

TAKE IT AWAY

The more you take away from
me, the bigger I will grow.

— WHAT AM I **?** —

Solution on p. 127

150

VANISHING HEAD

What loses its head in the morning
but gets it back again

— IN THE EVENING **?** —

Solution on p. 128

151

READY TO RACE

Forty rally cars line up at the start of a race.
Five percent of the cars carry one spare wheel.
Out of the 95 percent left, half carry two spare
wheels and half have no spare at all.

HOW MANY SPARE WHEELS ARE THERE IN TOTAL

 Solution on p. 128

152

PARKING PROBLEM

How many cars can you park
in an empty garage?

Professor's tip:
Remember that the garage
must be empty.

Solution on p. 128

UNFILLABLE

What is no bigger than a saucepan, can be held in
your hand like a saucepan, but no amount of water

___ **CAN FILL
IT UP ?** ___

Solution on p. 128

Sum Total

154

Complete the equation using the numbers
0–9 once (three has already been used):

$$3 \text{ x} \text{ - - - -} \text{ (4 digits)} = \text{ - - - - -} \text{ (5 digits)}$$

Solution on p. 128

155

OLD PALS

A man named George was walking through the downtown area when he bumped into an old college friend he hadn't seen for years.

They stopped and talked for awhile, catching up on old times.

"I married someone you don't know," said his friend, "and this is our daughter."

The little girl said hello to George, who asked her what her name was.

"It's the same as my mommy's," she replied.

"Then your name is Sarah!" said George.

— HOW DID HE KNOW —

Solution on p. 128

156

RICH AND POOR

Poor people have me, rich people need me,
and if you eat me, you will starve.

— WHAT AM I **?** —

Solution on p. 128

157

Missing Number

1, 11, 21, 1211, 111221, - - - - - -

Complete the sequence.

Solution on p. 128

158

HEADS AND FEET

A farmer has chickens roaming around a field where cows are grazing. He tries to count them. He counts 8 heads and 28 feet.

HOW MANY COWS DOES HE HAVE, AND HOW MANY CHICKENS?

Solution on p. 128

159

FATHERS AND SONS

A man joins a small group looking at a portrait. He studies the portrait for a moment and then says, "Brothers and sisters, I have none, but that man's father is my father's son."

WHO IS IN THE PORTRAIT?

Solution on p. 128

PARADISE ISLAND

Three sailors on a yacht approached a tropical island and spotted a beautiful beach, where they decided to spend a while lazing in the sunshine. They all dived into the water headfirst to swim ashore. None of them was wearing any kind of hat or swimming cap, and all of them went under the water before bobbing up to start swimming, but only two of them got their hair wet.

HOW COULD THIS BE **?**

Solution on p. 128

PUZZLES AND RIDDLES ANSWERS

1. Take the second glass, pour it into the fifth glass, and put it back.

2. Seven—there is only one brother, but he is brother to all of the girls.

3. Heartbeats.

4. Put five in the first cup, five in the second cup, and then put the second cup in the third cup.

5. They were playing different opponents.

6. Harry knows that the "apples and pears" label is wrong, so he picks one fruit from there. He then knows whether that box contains apples or pears and can put the correct label on it. If it was an apple, for instance, he can then transfer the "pears" label to the box that was marked "apples" and put the "apples and pears" label on the one that was marked "pears."

7. Kevin, Brian, Simon, Alan, Ian.

8. It wasn't raining.

9.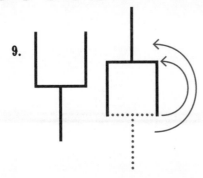

10. The girl has 7 and the boy has 5.

11. Mount Everest. It was still there, even though it hadn't been discovered.

12. Jump off the bottom rung.

13. Three to be sure, two if you're lucky.

14. There are four sequences:
192, 384, 576
219, 438, 657
273, 546, 819
327, 654, 981

15. They were grandfather, son, and grandson.

16. Two hours. James will eat 54 (27 per hour), Sarah will eat 24 (12 per hour), and Dominic will eat 42 (21 per hour).

17. Your tongue.

18. 301. If it chews through the first page of Vol. 1, then (not counting covers) it is straight onto the last page of Vol. 2. It goes all the way through Vol. 2 and stops at the last page of Vol. 3, which is next to the first page of Vol. 2.

19. Sawdust.

20. Blame.

21. They are two of triplets.

22. She gives ten children an apple and the eleventh child the bowl with the apple in it.

23. Footsteps.

24. None. All of the soil has been dug out of the hole.

25.

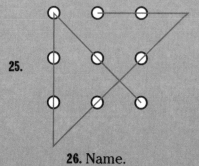

26. Name.

27.

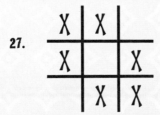

28. The answer is actually deceptively simple for anyone who has studied the radius and circumference of circles at school. The circumference of a circle is 2 x pi x radius. We take the value of pi to be 3.14. Because we are looking for the extra length of string we will need, we are calculating the difference between the first circumference (the string laid along the ground) and the second (the string held one foot from the ground). The difference between the first radius and the second is one foot, so the difference between the circumferences is:

2 x 3.14 x 1 foot = 6.28 feet

The second piece of string would have to be just 6.28 feet longer than the first.

29.

30.

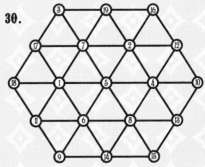

31. The parrot is deaf.

32. David.

33. $99 + (9 \div 9) = 100$

34. A mirror.

35.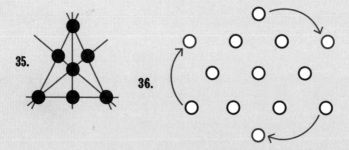

36.

37. Silence.

38. Most creatures. Buildings can't jump.

39. Stars.

40. None. The bigger ones would be willing to shake hands when they met a giant smaller than themselves, but the smaller ones would refuse.

41.

You need to think in 3-D and see this as a pyramid.

42. Skeleton Pete puts one gold doubloon into one chest and everything else in the other. When he is blindfolded, if he chooses the chest with the single gold doubloon, he has won, and if he chooses the other chest, he still has almost a 50 percent chance of winning.

43.

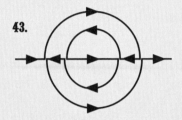

44. I am a girl—a daughter, not a son.

45. Darkness.

46. They are facing each other.

47. Second.

48. Someone's temper.

49. The shaggy barber. He must have cut the dapper barber's hair and done a good job, while the dapper barber must have cut the shaggy barber's hair.

50. 14.

51. His horse was named Friday.

52. Yesterday.

53.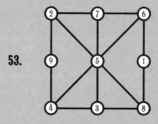

54. The stair carpet.

55. It is her fifteenth birthday.

56. Cut it in half in the normal way, then make another cut all the way across to cut it into quarters, then slice the cake in half horizontally.

57. An egg.

58. He's still alive—"living in Canada."

59. A secret.

60. The one with the biggest head.

61. The bus driver is walking.

62. Billy. Today must be Thursday.

63. An umbrella.

64. On a map.

65. On the sixteenth day.

66. The telephone.

67. O N D—they are the months of the year (October, November, December).

68. It is daytime.

69.

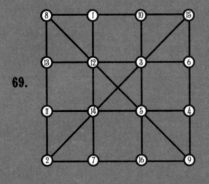

This is just one of many possible solutions.

70. It takes three turns. Turn three up. Turn two up and one down. Turn three up.

71. You could be incredibly lucky and pick out three matching pairs right away by choosing just six socks, but if you rule out chance altogether, you will have to pick out the 2 red socks, 4 yellow socks, and 5 of each of the other colors. You have now hauled 46 socks out of the drawer and need just one more to be sure of having 6 matching socks (three pairs), so the answer is 47.

72. Three; one in New York, one in Paris, and one in London.

73. Tilt the glass at an angle until the water is right at the lip of the glass, about to pour out. At this point, if it is touching the top edge at the bottom of the glass, then the glass is half full. If the water is only partway up the bottom of the glass, it is less than half full. If it is partway up the top edge of the glass, it is more than half full.

74. Are you asleep?

75. The door to the room.

76. L8—upside down these are the numbers from 86 to 91.

77. Thursday.

78. There are at least seven family members.

79. This is one of the oldest and most famous riddles of all time. The Sphinx is said to have guarded the entrance to the Greek city of Thebes, where he asked this riddle of travelers. Those who could not answer were eaten. The Greek hero, Oedipus, solved the riddle by answering: Man—who crawls on all fours as a baby, then walks on two feet as an adult, then uses a walking stick in old age.

80. He fills the 3-gallon bottle and pours it into the 5-gallon bottle. He then has 2 gallons of space left in the 5-gallon bottle. He fills the 3-gallon bottle again and uses it to fill up the 5-gallon bottle. Two gallons are used, leaving 1 gallon in the 3-gallon bottle.

81. He takes the chicken across, then he goes back. He takes the fox across, then takes the chicken back with him when he returns for the corn. He takes the corn across, leaving the chicken behind, and then goes back to pick up the chicken.

82. The man is a priest.

83. A bar of soap.

84. $IX - IV = V$

85. He is ten.

86. They are in different time zones. One of the sisters, for instance, could be in Los Angeles, and one could be in London. The boys were born at the same instant, yet the time difference between the two cities was such that their births were on different days.

87. Only one person, the original traveler, is guaranteed to be going to St. Ives. Everyone he meets could well be going the other way.

88. The Moon.

89. They were heading away from each other.

90.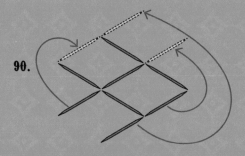

91. Your name.

92. The Sun.

93. 204—there are 64 single squares, one 8 x 8 square, four 7 x 7 squares, nine 6 x 6 squares, 16 5 x 5 squares, 25 4 x 4 squares, 36 3 x 3 squares, 49 2 x 2 squares.

94. Doing the sum in their head, most people end up with a total of 5,000, but the correct answer is actually 4,100.

95. Tomorrow.

96. Yes. You stop thinking of places to look once you have found it.

97. Your age.

98. The police officer is his mother.

99. A priest.

100. A hole.

101. The guard had been dreaming, so he was punished for being asleep on duty.

102. A promise.

103. Gloves.

104. A cold.

105. A piece from a jigsaw puzzle.

106. A melted snowman.

107. A breath.

108. Take each other's cars.

109. Warmth—you can easily catch a cold.

110. A stamp.

111.

1	2	20	23	19
3	25	4	12	21
22	18	13	5	7
24	6	11	16	8
15	14	17	9	10

112. A candle.

113. A towel.

114. There are 11 solutions:
123 + 45 - 67 + 8 - 9 = 100; 123 + 4 - 5 + 67 - 89 = 100;
123 - 45 - 67 + 89 = 100; 123 - 4 - 5 - 6 - 7 + 8 - 9 = 100;
12 + 3 + 4 + 5 - 6 - 7 + 89 = 100; 12 + 3 - 4 + 5 + 67 + 8 + 9 = 100;
12 - 3 - 4 + 5 - 6 + 7 + 89 = 100; 1 + 23 - 4 + 56 + 7 + 8 + 9 = 100;
1 + 23 - 4 + 5 + 6 + 78 - 9 = 100; 1 + 2 + 34 - 5 +67 - 8 + 9 = 100;
1 + 2 + 3 - 4 + 5 + 6 + 78 + 9 = 100

115. Fire.

116. An hourglass.

117. They are back to back.

118. Once. After that, you are subtracting 10 from 90 and so on.

119. Just one of these statements is true, the ninth one.

120. He can ask either one of them which way the other one would tell him to go. The liar will point him in the wrong direction. The truth-teller will also point him in the wrong direction, because that's where the liar would tell him to go. So he knows not to take the path that is pointed out to him, but to take the other one.

121.

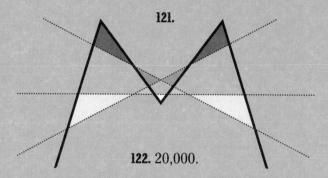

122. 20,000.

123. He was painting the window frames inside the house.

124. 45—one-fifth of 45 is 9, and 45 plus 9 is 54.

125. The third day after Wednesday is Saturday; therefore, the day after tomorrow is Saturday. That makes today Thursday, and the day before yesterday was Tuesday.

126. Turn over both hourglasses. Wait until the 7-minute hourglass runs out and then turn it over again. After four minutes, the 11-minute glass will run out, so you must immediately turn the 7-minute glass back again, since you know it has four minutes worth of sand in the bottom. When the 7-minute hourglass is empty, it will have timed four minutes on top of the 11 minutes from the other hourglass, making a total of 15 minutes.

127. A sponge.

128. A game of chess.

129. A computer keyboard.

130. Jane would know she was an eagle if Freddy and Mike both had bear buttons. She couldn't tell, therefore Freddy and Mike must either have an eagle and a bear or both have eagles. If Freddy had a bear, then Mike would know he had an eagle, but Mike can't tell. Freddy can be sure, therefore, that he is in The Eagle Team.

131. You can't dig half a hole.

132. Lewis Carroll based this riddle on Shakespeare's play *The Merchant of Venice*, where the moneylender Shylock demanded a pound of flesh from his victim if his debt was not paid. The legal judgment went against Shylock when he demanded the pound of flesh because he was allowed to take flesh but no blood. Most people would say that each of the pieces of stick should weigh a quarter of a pound, but they would actually weigh less because of the sawdust that was lost when they were cut. Like Shylock overlooking the blood, everyone overlooks the sawdust.

133. A snail.

134. E N T (they are the first letters of the numbers ONE to TEN).

135. Icicles.

136. There were no stairs because it is a single story house.

137. He throws it up in the air.

138. A clock.

139. 20

140.

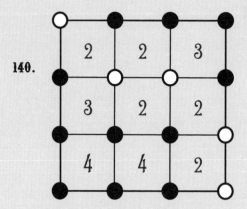

141. Yesterday, today, and tomorrow.

142. The only place in the world where the man could run south, west, then north, and end up back where he started is at the North Pole.

The most likely color for the bear is, therefore, white, since it would be a polar bear.

143. 888 + 88 + 8 + 8 + 8 = 1,000

144. All seven are girls.

145. 6,210,001,000

146. He told one child to divide the land into two sections and to give the other child first choice.

147. A key.

148. Twice. Load the balance once with two selections of three balls, leaving three aside. If one of the selections is heavier, the heavy ball is one of those three. If both selections weigh exactly the same, the heavy ball is one of the three set aside. You have now established which of the sets of three contains the heavy ball. Load the scales a second time, placing one of the suspect balls on each side and leaving one out. If one of the balls on the scales is heavier, it will be obvious, and if they both weigh the same, then the heavy ball is the one you left out.

149. A hole.

150. A pillow.

151. 40.

152. One. After that, it is no longer an <u>empty</u> garage.

153. A colander.

154. 3 x 5,694 = 17,082

155. His old college friend was a woman named Sarah.

156. Nothing.

157. 312211 (three ones, two twos, one one)

158. Six cows and two chickens.

159. His son.

160. One of them was bald.

Professor's tip:
Finished already? How many did you get right? No doubt you found some more difficult than others——not everyone is good at solving the same types of puzzles or riddles. Whichever ones were your favorites, I hope you had a brain-busting good time!